SUPER BLOOM

Photographs by
Michael Lee Jackson

Room With a View Press
255 Great Arrow Avenue, Suite 204
Buffalo, New York 14207

Cover & Layout by Paul Marko/Download Design

www.MichaelLeeJackson.com
©2020 Michael Lee Jackson. All rights reserved.

Contents

Acknowledgements — iv

Introduction — v

Images — 1

Postscript — 87

About the Photographer — 89

Acknowledgements

Very special thanks to my mum, Susan Halpern, my father, Bruce Jackson, my fairy godmother, Diane Christian, my dear friends and family who took a look at this and convinced me it was worth finishing. Thanks to Jessica Jackson and Chris LaLonde for the great suggestions and Rachel Jackson for the constant support and encouragement, and Dimitri Hamlin for the eagle eyes on a few of these images.

Big thanks to Kristine Hornung Pottle, Barry Covert, Jennifer Wolfe, Kirk Siegler, Ari Hodosh, and my other friends and family out there who have supported and encouraged these quixotic endeavors over the years, and thanks to Jim Nilzon for taking the picture of me at the end of this book.

Introduction

The Carrizo Plain National Monument is only about a hundred miles north of Los Angeles, as the crow flies, and about sixty miles east of Bakersfield. Despite its proximity to Los Angeles, few people I know in Los Angeles, even most of the lifers I know, have ever heard of it or been there. The Carrizo Plain is the largest remaining natural grassland in California at 40 miles in length from north to south and framed by the Caliente mountains to the west and the Temblor mountains to the east. I came across it late one night when looking on Google Earth for places to explore within a few hours of Los Angeles.

Part of the San Andreas fault is visible on the Carrizo Plain. There are petroglyphs from the Chumash, Salinan and Yokuts peoples at a beautiful sandstone horseshoe shaped area called Painted Rock, now hard to get in to because of vandals. But lest you think that vandalism is a recent thing, there is American graffiti in the cave there dating back to the early 1900's, and Portuguese engravings going back to the 1800's. Even some old vandalism becomes important historically, but that's another discussion. There are remnants of old ranches from the homesteading days, abandoned trailers that look like *Breaking Bad* sets, an abandoned boat, a well-protected grave site, and plenty of dirt roads to explore and views to discover.

I've been going to the Carrizo Plain for ten years or so. I love it in all its incarnations. Even when it looks burned out and the visitors have predominantly left for the year, awaiting the next time the monument is on the front page of national newspapers or featured on cable news for its fabulous blooms, I love it. In fact, I used an image from one of those burned-looking fields on the back cover of my CD *Death by Sunshine* a few years back. I love the solitude, the quiet, the space, and I've learned that when I stop, look and listen, the Carrizo Plain is like a mini Serengeti. There are herds of deer and pronghorns, rabbits, coyotes, foxes, hawks, buzzards, and many other birds, and when the flowers are blooming in the spring it's hard not to hear the sounds of bees buzzing about. There's life everywhere there year-round, and to see it one just has to be quiet and pay attention.

Exploring the Carrizo Plain and surrounding areas during a super bloom is like being inside a giant watercolor painting. Super blooms happen there and in nearby places like Antelope Valley and Death Valley on those years when southern California has had proper winters with considerable rain over time, not just the kind of storms when an atmospheric river comes by and deluges the area, but the steadier rains that actually have a chance of being absorbed by the ground. The winter of 2018/2019 was such a year for the Carrizo Plain.

The 2019 bloom lasted a month or so, which is much longer than the previous years I'd been there. Other than these occasional few weeks, the Carrizo Plain looks golden, dry, and sparse on a quick glance, as it does in the last photograph of this book. The occasional transformation to a 250,000-acre watercolor painting is an astonishing thing to behold, as is the transformation back.

When it blooms, the mostly dormant flowers in the area explode, and suddenly one can see the full color spectrum in the flowers which include, among many others, Clovers, Fiddle Neck, Alfalfa, Small Melilot, Deer Weed, Costa-Bird's-foot Trefoil, Reddish Tufted Vetch, San Joaquin Milkvetch, Padre's Shooting Star, various Gilia, various Linanthus, Blazing Stars, Baby Blue Eyes, various Phacelia, Purple Wild Onion, Milkweed, Douglas' Stitchwort, Colorado Four O'clock, Alkali Heath, Gypsum Spring Beauty, various Lupines, Thistles, Silver Puffs, Dandelions, Goldfields, Sunflowers, and Daisies.

A Dream

A while back I reconnected with an old friend in Buffalo, New York, one who'd always marveled at my peregrinations, and she would ask what I was running from. At this first hang out in probably a decade or more, she marveled again and asked the same old question. I had an answer this time: I told her I was afraid to stop, that I would atrophy if I did. It was at least partially true. That afternoon I took a nap and had a dream that I was driving in Patagonia. It was so beautiful. There were volcanic lakes and ponds, large and small, extraordinary wildlife I'd never seen before and which my imagination had put together in the dream, the birds, sky, and light. It was wonderous and I was looking for a place to pull over so I could photograph this dream vision of Patagonia. Then the road started to climb and quickly got incredibly steep. I got scared and slowed down, thinking I should turn around, but as I looked in my rear-view mirror, I realized that if I even slowed down, I would fall off the mountain. I was terrified. But I had no choice but to keep going, I could barely see the top in the distance and had no idea if it led to something even more deadly, like a road going down at the same pitch.

And that was how the dream ended, with me crawling up a hill in 4-wheel drive low, hoping my car wouldn't just fall off the mountain.

What's the connection? Well, one day early in March 2019 when I was driving north on Soda Lake Road at the Carrizo Plain, I noticed one of the occasional dirt roads that goes to the east toward the Temblor mountain range. Before the Temblors there were some foothills that the road appeared to go over, steeply I might add. But not as steep as the road down on the other side, I later learned. Like a moth to a flame, I dropped the truck into 4-wheel drive and crawled up the hill. When I got to the top I was rewarded with a stunning view in every direction. There was a water tower that had some gorgeous artwork etched into it. I love that someone took the time to make art in a place few would ever see. And then came the road down toward Elkhorn road and the Temblors. That road was narrow and steep.

Not nearly as steep as my scary dream, but just the same, I am terrified of heights and I wasn't about to stop and hope that the emergency brake would hold my truck in place while I took some photos. In an odd way, I think that dream motivated me to explore the kind of roads there (and elsewhere) that'd I'd previously been afraid to explore.

As I would soon learn, that was one of the more benign roads I drove at the Carrizo Plain in 2019. That day I discovered for myself a part of the park I'd never seen. I suppose I could have asked someone how to get over to the Temblors, but I never did. I'd come home from some of my Carrizo Plain trips, look at Google Maps and think about it, but yet always drove familiar and safe routes up and down Soda Lake Road, exploring only the Caliente mountains to the west. During blooms I now find myself more interested in the nooks and crannies of the Temblor range, though to see much of it, you need a capable high clearance 4x4 to get in and out, and it's very much worth hiking the canyons.

An Explorer and Chasing Rainbows

The same day that I chanced on toward the Temblors there were great clouds to the east, what appeared to be a storm system coming in from the north, and gorgeous sunlight sneaking out from the south. As you will see from the photographs in this collection, I'm particularly drawn to cloudy scenery with sunlight coming in from behind me. That kind of light bounces down from the sky with all the harshness beautifully filtered out and the bright sky turned down a few notches. My step mum, Diane Christian, calls this Venetian light. It's my favorite light for almost all the photography I do. Everything is airbrushed in that light. Nature's filters are the best. Some of my photographer friends now call it "MJ light."

As I headed north on Elkhorn road, I encountered a tall scruffy-looking guy named Bill Johnson standing by a 4-wheel drive pickup truck with a pop-up camper in the bed and a dog named Bosco in the back seat. Bill was standing alongside the road staring north with a concerned expression on his face, an iPad in his hand and scratching his beard. I pulled up and asked, "You ok?" He said, "Yeah, thanks, I'm checking weather radar and am a little concerned about the storm coming in from the north, there is a heavy rain cell headed our way. If I get stuck in here, I'll not only miss the game this evening, but my wife won't be too happy because we are planning to visit her mother tomorrow."

Having been in that area before when it rained, I knew what he was talking about. The dust turns into a mud more difficult than any snow or ice I've ever encountered–and I'm from Buffalo, New York. Even with a vehicle that can handle anything, unless you've got chains on, driving is nearly impossible when those roads get wet. I can't imagine it's very navigable even with chains.

Bill continued, "I was hoping to get to that spot called "Where God Spilled His Paint" today but I don't know if that's going to work out." I'd heard of that place. It's the name given to a place where an iconic picture of the park was taken by a photographer named Frankie Kee in 2005 after what must have been a very wet winter. Bill said he hadn't seen the park as colorful since the spring after a wildfire burned much of the area a few decades prior. Bill was kind enough to share with me what he believed to be the "Where God Spilled His Paint" GPS coordinates as I mulled going for it. I managed to get the coordinates in to my phone with minimal signal so I had some idea where I was going.

I thanked Bill, wished him well and headed north in search of a place I would soon learn is more mythical than real. It started to rain, and the rain was getting more intense. Even though I almost always have enough provisions for a few days when I go into remote places, I thought better of it in this case and turned around. I came upon Bill again who'd figured he'd give it a shot too. He said, "If you're turning around and driving that thing (a Toyota 4Runner TRD Pro), I'll turn around too, I reckon." One of us suggested we get a bite in Taft, an oil town just to the east of the Temblors. We ended up at a cheap and cheerful Mexican restaurant that was my local for the evenings I stayed in Taft. I learned that Bill is a junior high school teacher. He takes the families of his students on outdoor activities once a month and was scouting the area for a planned trip to the Carrizo Plain with parents the next weekend to camp and visit the super bloom. In his off time, Bill likes to truly get lost, the more remote and fewer people the better. I understand.

When I say the place called "Where God Spilled His Paint" is mythical, that isn't to say that the photograph by Kee isn't real. By all accounts I could find it is, and I've seen places in the park that look like that, so I have no reason to doubt its authenticity. But what I mean is that in the best of super bloom years, the blooms are temporary and are largely dictated by environmental conditions like temperature, sunlight, and precipitation, and the area is in a constant flux between the life cycles of the flowers and light.

During my quest to find that mythical spot last year, I quickly realized the futility of those efforts. When I got to where I'm fairly sure that photograph was taken it just didn't look like that at all, and that was in the middle of an epic super bloom. I thought I recognized the topography, but those colors weren't there at that time. Other parts of the park and surrounding areas were much more beautiful to me. But it was also futile for other reasons. The beauty in the Carrizo plain is everywhere and totally subjective in all instances. I've learned that when wandering through a rainbow, I should just search until I find what pleases my senses the most.

I found some truly stunning views there in the spring of 2019. Few were places anyone suggested I go. There were no signs, frequently no roads and often no trails. And that was the joy of the 2019 super bloom for me. It was about exploration, discovery, pushing myself and pushing boundaries, both physical and geographical.

Kirk Siegler, an NPR reporter and friend, was emotionally drained from reporting on the horrific Camp wildfire in northern California in late 2018 and asked me to take him out to the Carrizo Plain to do a story about the super bloom. Flowers, he thought, would be a pleasant respite from loss and destruction. It was April 19, 2019 when we went which is late in the season for the flowers in that area. There wasn't much left, but I took Kirk to the most colorful places I'd found. They were mostly golden brown by that point, still beautiful, but not the rainbow they'd offered in the preceding days and weeks.

On one of the back roads in the Temblor mountains, we came upon a family driving through in a vehicle I was confident would end up with a broken axle up there. A woman in the car asked me, "Where is the best place?" The question didn't make sense to me. I replied "I don't know. You have to find the best spot for you, which might not be what anyone else thinks is the best spot, whatever that is." She looked at me quizzically. I urged her to keep her eyes on the ground when walking around there as the rattlesnakes were out to bring a lot of water, cautions I am certain were ignored. I know they didn't break an axle up there as we saw them again a few hours later on the northern stretch of Elkhorn road, near Wallace Creek continuing their quest to find the "best place" and fully ignoring my cautions about water and snakes.

The Purple River and Other Attempts to Get Inside the Watercolor

There is a sliver of purple flowers that tends to run north and south through the middle of the Carrizo Plain in wet years. Getting to it eluded me for a while. I couldn't find the right dirt road or path to get to them, if there was one. One year I parked somewhere I thought reasonable to the west and began walking east toward the 'purple river' as I call it. The thing about big places is that everything is farther away than it appears. As I walked through the knee-deep grass toward the purple river, like that scene in Monty Python's "Holy Grail" when the guards of the castle were facing an attack, the purple river just seemed to always be the same distance away. I was soaked from all the moisture in the plants and at what seemed like a mile or so in, I finally gave up and went back, mumbling to myself "Camelot is a silly place…" My dog Shadow loved it though and bounced around like a gazelle in there. Normally that area is quite full of rattlesnakes, but that day was pretty cold, so I wasn't very worried about the snakes.

In the spring of 2019, I finally found a dirt road that went to the south end of the purple river. There were a few spots that were difficult to navigate because of mud and water and tumbleweeds, but I eventually got to that spot that had eluded me so. As beautiful as it is, it's more beautiful from a few miles back where you can actually see the scope of it. But I had to get close to know that, and this is a lesson I learned a few times there in 2019.

I sent a copy of the picture of the purple river (page 4) to Ian Gillan, singer for *Deep Purple* and a good friend. He wrote back in his own inimitable prose:

> *That's a beautiful picture, not just because of nature's splendour, but you've taken the viewer to a special place.*
>
> *I really do love it, not least because of the mood-matching image that fits right in with a lyrical scenario I'm sketching in the middle of this night for a DP idea we'll be recording soon.*
>
> *Now, I'm supposed to get back to sleep with the vison of pre-Raphaelite nubiles in translucent robes, skipping through a valley of bluebells to the sound of a DP rehearsal track that's driving me nuts …*
>
> *Cheers, IG*

I've Got to Work Harder

Another day while exploring in the hills off Elkhorn road, I'd gone up a dirt road that would soon be fenced off with "No Trespassing" signs as word got out about the bloom and the park got crowded. I'd parked the car and was looking over a barbed wire fence toward yellow, purple and orange covered hills that looked like candy and were so inviting. I was concerned that the land on the other side of the fence was private property, but so eagerly wanted to climb those mountains and walk the valleys below as well.

It was then that I saw a guy walking out of the canyon. I waved hello as people tend to do out there. I asked if it was private property. He said it wasn't and came to the fence to explain. He said it was public BLM land and that the fence was an old homestead era ranching fence. He was wearing rubber boots that went up to just below his knees, for the rattlesnakes, he said. He explained that he was a photographer, and said he'd been trudging his way through all the canyons I'd been eyeing from the dirt roads above. I asked him how he got into those canyons and got around. He said, "oh, I just bushwhacked my way through…" He showed me some of his pictures on his Fuji medium format camera and they were astonishingly beautiful on the screen in that bright light. I knew I had to work harder if I wanted to get pictures that had the same impact on others as his work impacted me. And so, I did.

I lifted up the barbed wire and went underneath with Shadow and held it up for my friend, Natalia Bruschi, who was exploring with me that day. The guy we'd just met told me it was really pretty a few valleys over from where we could see from that vantage point.

I went back a few more times, climbed those mountains, and made my way into some of the canyons as well. Bill Johnson inspired me to get a Garmin hand-held satellite navigation and communicator, which I used to drop markers where I left my car and for some of the spots I loved. I brought a tripod and used it and some of my favorite pictures in this collection are from those hikes, inspired to work harder by a stranger who's name I don't even know. No trails. No people. No signs. It was difficult, hot as hell, sublime, and worth it. Thank you, stranger.

Swarm!

On April 4, 2019 while walking down a mountain at the Carrizo Plain with Natalia and my friend and client, Simon Fawcett, we started to hear a distant low frequency hum, like a generator running far away. Only it was getting closer and louder. Natalia, who was lagging behind yelled "swarm!" as the noise got louder and louder. I turned around and close behind her was a cloud of bees coming our way. I yelled "They're just working and won't hurt you. Turn around and cover your head…" and then I did the same. The cloud of bees must have taken ten or fifteen seconds to pass us. We got pelted by a few as they went by, but there were no injuries and not a single sting.

What a gorgeous phenomenon.

Go Further. Just Don't Follow Me.

Kirk and I covered quite a lot of ground in our day and a half drive about the Carrizo Plain. I remember telling him I wish more people would just explore off the beaten path, challenge themselves more, learn more, experience more and that perhaps through that experience gain and share a deeper respect for the importance of preserving nature. He joked "Go further…, just don't follow me." I laughed and said, "Yeah, I guess you're right" because the truth is, I like being alone out there. And if anyone followed me, I'd just have to go farther, which I suppose wouldn't be so bad if not for the fact that it's getting harder and harder to truly get lost.

It's a conundrum for me, because at the same time I want people to explore more, I want those places to remain pristine and those two objectives can be mutually exclusive. I guess the middle ground for me is to share the beauty with images, and to hopefully encourage leaving no trace, and the preservation and responsible enjoyment of those places. So perhaps I should change the heading above to "Go Further, Don't Do Anything Stupid, and Leave No Trace." Doesn't quite have the same ring to it, though, does it?

In all seriousness, if you haven't been to the Carrizo Plain and decide to go, please plan smart. Bring more food and water than you think you need, as you might get stuck. There are no services there. Bring extra clothes to keep you warm and dry. You may not have cell phone coverage in much of the monument. The roads are almost entirely dirt and get very dusty when dry and extremely slippery when wet, so drive slowly and considerately. Know when to turn around before you're stuck. And whatever you do, be careful, and do your best to leave this magical place as you found it.

Organization.

All the pictures in this book, except for the last two, were taken in and around the Carrizo Plain in March and early April 2019. The final two pictures were taken in late February 2020. The final image before the back cover on page 85 is the same area which appears in full bloom on the cover and on page 27.

I was at a loss as to how to organize these photos for this collection. Ultimately, it made the most sense to me to present them chronologically so viewers could see some of the arc of change over my ten visits between March 15 and April 19, 2019 and my visit in February 2020.

Particularly toward the later visits, you'll notice it starting to look more burned out with only the yellow remaining vibrant. This was particularly so on the eastern side of the Carrizo Plain toward and into the Temblor Mountains. Even on my final 2019 visit, there were still some beautiful multi-colored flowers blooming on the west side in the step hills of the Caliente Mountains.

Not quite the end.

So, I thought I was done shooting the photos for this book and that I'd surely get it done in the summer of 2019, but life happens. Things get in the way. Priorities get bumped and we get distracted. Fast forward to February 2020. Covid-19 was well along its journey through the world. California was starting to shut down, though the state of emergency wasn't declared until early March. Many of the people I knew were starting to be genuinely afraid, and rightly so. It occurred to me that I didn't have the last few shots of the book, which should be pictures of the Carrizo Plain, preferably pictures of spots I'd photographed in full bloom, looking as they do the rest of the time. I headed back and felt as though I had the entire place to myself. I don't recall seeing anyone in there on that drive. The last two pictures in this book are from that jaunt.

When the California state-wide stay-at-home order was issued March 19, 2020 to try and slow the spread of Covid-19, I suddenly had a lot more time on my hands, and no excuse not to finish this book. Even with that resolve, it takes some time. See the postscript for more.

Michael Lee Jackson
Socially distanced, in between here and there,
October, 2020

Postscript

A few words about color.

Unless you're into graphic design, printing, and photography geekdom, the following may bring tears of boredom to your eyes. You've been warned.

My lessons on the journey that inspired this book did not end with editing the pictures after each trip to the Carrizo Plain.

Until this book I never gave much thought about the fact that when one prints a book, there is a need to convert from the RGB color space on our computers, which have a nearly infinite palate of gradations and nuance to please our eyes and match what our brain does when we input color, to CMYK. There's a big difference between what a computer and monitor can do and what physical printers can do.

I never worried about it because ignorance is bliss. Other people always handled these mysterious conversions without me ever needing to know. I'd see the proofs of album covers, posters, or whatever it may have been and sometimes opine that one of the colors might be more saturated to match what I'd signed off on originally, but that was about it. When the Shadow book came out in 2017, I thought the colors were ok, but I knew they weren't as brilliant as what I'd been looking at on my screen. I didn't know that Alex Bitterman, who had helped with the design and layout of the book had converted the RGB TIFF files I sent him using a proprietary conversion profile he'd put together to best replicate colors in the projects he works on. Why would I have known? I got my proof and was so excited to see the book taking shape I quickly disabused myself of the memories of exactly how those images were colored on my monitor. It was close enough and beyond good enough.

But this book is about flowers. It's all about the color, colors I bathed in when I took these photos. This book is because of the colors.

As I was putting this book together in February 2020 I spoke to another friend, Kristin Bedford, who was then also preparing a book for a major photography publisher and press. She said she was agonizing over the CMYK conversions. I had no idea what she was talking about and thought she was being OCD in all the time and money she was putting into that process. "Just send your book off..." is what I thought. I've since learned that part of the reason *National Geographic*, for example, is so gorgeous is because they have dedicated people to oversee the conversions from RGB (or whatever the initial color space is) to CMYK for printing. There are people who make a living doing just that, and were there any real budget for this book, I'd surely have hired one of them rather than suffer this process. I'd have more hair if I did.

I talked to a bunch of people, including Alex and John Greene, the owner of K.D. Press who printed this book, and found out that I did have to do these conversions, or someone would. So I took the first image in the book and did a conversion from RGB to CMYK in Photoshop. I have no idea which default profile it used. I wanted to die when I saw the CMYK version. It was crap. Dull colors, the blacks weren't black enough and almost everything I loved about that image seemed muted. I was stuck for a while on this conundrum.

And then John Greene kindly did a conversion on my draft and sent me a proof to see what it would look like if batch converted from RGB to CMYK using a common profile for his printers. At first, I thought they looked good, good enough. I expected some degradation of the richness and saturation, but it looked light years better than my original attempt. Then I looked back at the originals and much of the nuance, the richness of the colors and darkness of the blacks was not as good as I knew it could be with individual attention to each image. John was kind enough to tell me the CMYK profile his printers use (and which he used on my proofs). My friend, Paul Marko, who's helped with the layout and design of this book took a shot at the conversion of one of the images and sent it to me. I found myself immediately bitching to him about the greens not looking right, the blues, the purple wasn't purple, the poppies didn't look right... He suggested, quite correctly and reasonably, that the only way I could approach being happy with this output would be to do it myself with his help on the back end of that. So with a few pointers from Paul and hours of tutorials and instructional videos online, I dove in to Photoshop more deeply than I ever have (or ever wanted to), doing my best to bring out the nuances of these photos that made me choose them in the first place. I've had to drop childhood memories to make room for learning this process – even in the most basic entry-level way. In the entire process, there was only one image from the original draft which I couldn't get happy with and dropped from this collection. I have no doubt that this is due to the pilot not knowing how to fly the plane, and that with more skill and patience I could have saved it, but at this point I'm comfortable with that decision and think the collection is better without that image, which would have annoyed me every time I saw it.

So this book has been a journey in more ways than one. Beyond all the driving, hiking, camping and trekking around the Carrizo Plain coming home filthy, exhausted and covered in pollen, I've learned, that my job isn't nearly done when I've taken, edited, selected and organized a group of photos with a forward that tells the story. Without taking the time to do the color work, I'd have been walking away from finishing what I started, one of the most important parts of it, which would then undermine all that work in the first place. Another lesson, and I'm thankful for it. And maybe someday, when I have the time, I'll dig in further to the science of color, as I'm now more fascinated and vexed than ever by color, how we see it, process it, and reproduce it in different media.

Onward.

About the Photographer

Michael Lee Jackson is a photographer, musician, and attorney.

Jackson spends a considerable amount of time on backroads chasing light and taking photographs. His landscape photography has been shown in exhibits in Los Angeles, California, and Buffalo, New York.

With his musical groups, Jackson has toured the world extensively and released numerous records. In 1999, he toured with 10,000 Maniacs. In 2005, Jackson began working with Ian Gillan, the singer for Deep Purple, as creative manager, guitar player and music director for two records, one DVD and a north American tour in 2006. In the last few years Jackson released the records *"Death by Sunshine"* (2017) and *"Satisfaction Garage"* (2020), and he re-released the records *"Dawn"* and *"Toast"* (2019).

As an attorney, Jackson concentrates on drafting and negotiating contracts as well as working on intellectual property-related matters for a variety of clients in the entertainment industry. During law school and for some years afterwards, Jackson worked with civil rights attorneys William Kunstler (who convinced Jackson to go to law school) and Ron Kuby. In 1998, Jackson received a Thurgood Marshall award for representing an indigent person pro bono in a capital case.

Jackson has written three books, *"Your Father's Not Coming Home Anymore"* (co-author Jessica Jackson) (1982), *"Doing Drugs"* (1983), and the photography book, *"Shadow"* (2017).

Photo by Bruce Jackson